ABOVE THE STORM CLOUDS

A DISCIPLING GUIDE FOR EMPOWERING
CHRISTIAN BELIEVERS

WILLIAM H. MCINTYRE

Copyright © 2022 by William H. McIntyre.

ISBN 978-1-64133-773-1 (softcover)
ISBN 978-1-64133-774-8 (ebook)

All rights reserved. No part of this book may be reproduced or transmitted in any form or by any means, electronic or mechanical, including photocopying, recording, or by any information storage and retrieval system without express written permission from the author, except in the case of brief quotations embodied in critical reviews and certain other noncommercial uses permitted by copyright law.

Printed in the United States of America.

Brilliant Books Literary
137 Forest Park Lane Thomasville
North Carolina 27360 USA

Contents

Preface v
1. In the Beginning 1
2. The Wandering Years 11
3. Entering in by Grace 25
4. Proceeding Onward in Faith 41
5. Gaining Strength within God's Calling 51
6. Encouragement, Counselling, and Discipleship 57
7. The Priorities That Remain 63
8. The Home Stretch in Sight 69
9. The Final Victory 73
Appendix 77

PREFACE

This book was inspired by the rapidly deteriorating social issues and political unrest in America and throughout the world, exacerbated by the COVID 19 pandemic, which has caused many people to stop attending Christian churches due to fear, apathy or lack of knowledge. The Bible states in Hebrews 13:8 that "Jesus Christ is the same yesterday, today, and forever." He has not changed and still loves all people who, through faith, have received Him as Savior and Lord. God our creator, has provided everything needed for us to live happy, abundantly fulfilled lives and communicates with us through His Word. He will never leave us nor forsake us, and will bless us with good times while lovingly guiding us during difficult times as we communicate with Him through prayer! The Book of Acts tells us that the Holy Spirit was sent to earth as the comforter for His people and He remains active to this day to inspire, empower, and illuminate Scripture for their understanding! Therefore, this book is prayerfully offered by faith to renew hope and restore confidence in the inspired word of Almighty God, the close fellowship of Jesus His Son, and in the supernatural power of the Holy Spirit!

CHAPTER 1

IN THE BEGINNING

"In the beginning, God created the heavens and the earth" (Gen. 1:1 NIV). Thus, the world came into being. After the creation of the trees and other vegetation, the animals, the birds, and the fish of the sea, God shaped man out of the dust of the ground. When he had breathed life into man and then created woman for man, he blessed them and told them to be fruitful and increase in number.

This was the beginning of paradise for humankind. But to allow them to enjoy genuine fellowship, thank and praise him, and enjoy his presence by their own free will, God made people unhindered and independent. Yet in their own strength, they proved they were unable to keep their attention fixed on their creator. However, this independence opened the door for the first man and woman to become Satan's central focus.

Historically, unless an individual has been in a position of either pressure or temptation, he or she has not come near reaching his or her full potential. In certain instances, during such pressures or temptations, some decidedly wrong choices are made, which have profound lifetime impacts. While patience in making correct choices has provided peace and contentment, hastily or impulsively made choices have oftentimes been incorrect, yielding much distressing heartache.

The first man and woman mentioned in the Bible could have become complacent and might have started taking things for granted. Life for them was rich and full. Pain, sorrow, and discomfort were not really part of their experience in this God-created paradise.

As they walked in complete obedience with God, they enjoyed his close fellowship and reassuring voice. Therefore, when a temptation was subtly presented to them, they were mentally unprepared, having never experienced the consequences of sin. They had no reference point to determine the hidden result waiting for them, even though they both knew that giving in to the enticing offer would be disobeying God. This first act of man's rebellion towards God was recorded to allow all future generations to better understand the awful price sin demands. The paradise that people had come to enjoy was no longer available, and they began to experience mental and physical pain, and substantial hardship, previously unknown to them. Through this wrong choice, the fallen angel Lucifer (or Satan) appeared to have gained a victory.

Where was God during this time? Could he not have rescued them before it was too late? Yes, of course he could have. However, fully comprehending the human will in the face of constant enticements and temptations, he had an eternally perfect plan in mind to be accomplished by his own son. Adam and Eve were examples to the rest of humankind regarding sin and its consequences, yet we continue to see sin all around us to this present day.

Sin has blinded people throughout the ages. Even though the Old Testament records how God continued to send prophets and witnesses bearing the truth of his love, concern and compassion, humankind would not heed their message.

The marvelous truth that his love for humankind has never wavered, regardless of how greedy, self-centered, and despicable people were, certainly transcends mortal comprehension. At the appropriate time, his perfect plan regarding the birth, life, death, and resurrection of Jesus Christ, was put into motion and completed in its entirety.

However, until that appointed hour was to come, much world history had to take place. This history has been carefully recorded in the Old Testament books of Genesis through Malachi, with cross-references throughout the New Testament. Within these historical documents, a distinct bloodline manifested itself from book to book, leading to the final atonement at the cross of Calvary.

Modern humans are not much different from many of those described in the Old Testament, and remain without excuse for their ignorance of the spiritual realities set before them. Since sin entered the world by Satan's lie and man's acceptance of it, sin can only be dealt with by man's repentance and the cleansing power of the blood shed during Christ's death at Calvary. Faith is the only means whereby this truth can be apprehended.

People have had every opportunity to understand the two choices they have: to continue in sin which leads to eternal death, or receive pardon for their sins by accepting as savior and Lord, Jesus Christ, who then begins ushering in the tremendous benefits of eternal life.

What inhibits humans from reaching such an obvious conclusion? Ignorance, pride, and self-sufficiency are a few reasons. But of even more sincere concern is the ever-present whisperings of their old enemy, Satan. However, God's Holy Spirit is also present and available to all who want help. We need only to ask and he will respond.

The devil will fight and not give up easily. However, he knows he is a defeated foe and that God has the greater power.

Remember, "The Lord is not slow in keeping his promise, as some understand slowness. He is patient with you, not wanting anyone to perish, but everyone to come to repentance" (2 Pet. 3:9 NIV).

The forty books of the Old Testament encompass many generations of peoples and happenings, and reveal how humans have been constantly directed by spiritual influences.

During Old Testament times, though, there was never a lasting victory or peace because the religious leaders could only offer a temporary atonement through the blood of animals.

In Exodus 29:21, we see where the blood of a ram was sprinkled on the robes and bodies of Aaron and his sons. Various Bible commentaries clarify this by stating that the blood on their bodies and garments served to make the awfulness of sin and its penalty more vivid. It was visible evidence that life had been taken away and God's law vindicated. Every sacrifice testified of the offeror's surrender of the guilty to God and his service, and deep humility and gratefulness to the victim which became the substitute. Such animal sacrifices always pointed ahead to the final sacrifice accomplished at Calvary.

God purposely used these Old Testament men and women and their experiences to comfort, encourage, and give prophetic direction, while at the same time demonstrating his judgment for the wicked and disobedient. Therefore, modern humans need the Old Testament teachings to establish much of who and what God is, and to impart a clearer understanding regarding the greatness of his blessings.

From Isaiah 57, we learn that God is

> longsuffering and patient with those in rebellion; is faithful to warn men of the evil results of rebellion; predicts blessings to those who trust in him; is the High and Lofty One;

he inhabits eternity; his name is Holy; he dwells in a high and holy place; he also dwells with the contrite and humble and promises to revive them; he will not contend forever; he is not always angry; he retires from wrongdoing; he created the souls of men; and he will heal, revive, restore comforts, and create peace in the righteous, but permit the wicked to suffer loss of these things. (Isaiah 57 NKJV)

There are numerous titles given describing the characteristics of God to further help us know who he is. These titles, used many times throughout the Old Testament, were given so that humans could more easily grasp the fullness, all-encompassing majesty, and greatness of God our Heavenly Father. Some of the more important Hebrew names are as follows.

Jehovah-Elohim—The Eternal Creator
Adonai-Jehovah—The Lord our Sovereign; Master Jehovah
Jehovah-Jireh—The Lord will see or provide
Jehovah-Nissim—The Lord our banner
Jehovah-Ropheka—The Lord our healer
Jehovah-Shalom—The Lord our peace
Jehovah-Tsidkeenu—The Lord our righteousness
Jehovah-Mekaddishkem—The Lord our sanctifier
Jehovah-Saboath—The Lord of hosts
Jehovah-Shammah—The Lord is present
Jehovah-Elyon—The Lord most high
Jehovah-Rohi—The Lord my shepherd
Jehovah-Hoseenu—The Lord our maker

Jehovah-Eloheenu—The Lord our God
Jehovah-Eloheka—The Lord your God
Jehovah-Elohay—The Lord my God

Many more names and titles are used for God the Father in both the Old and New Testaments, with over 100 used to identify Jesus his son. Through these we can relate to God in every area of our lives, whether during times of joy and jubilation, or depression, sadness, pain, and sorrow.

When we examine the literal meaning of the names of the various Old Testament people and places, we learn much about the characteristics and personalities involved. For example,

Isaac means "laughter"
Esau - "hairy"
Judah - "praise"
Dinah - "vindicated"
Peniel (the place where Jacob wrestled with God) - "face of God"

When God gave Jacob his new name Israel, the stigma of "cheater" was replaced with "prince with God" or "God's prince."

In the New Testament Book of Hebrews, chapter 11, a number of important individuals of the Old Testament are listed regarding their strong faith—faith that led to miracle after miracle. Here we read about

Abel - "faith's worship"
Enoch - "faith's walk"
Noah - "faith's work"
Abraham - "faith's obedience"
Sara - "faith's reckoning"

This legacy of faith, handed down to God's followers, provides strong justification for them to emulate during their years here on earth. Repeatedly, persistent faith paid off in miraculous circumstances, which changed the course of history and led people on correct paths for a time. Nevertheless, when greed, envy, lust, and self-sufficiency crept in, people turned from following God and were soon living in defeat once again. Lesson after lesson is graphically described for all humankind to heed. Why then do people continue to succumb to the pressures and temptations of life, rather than turn and flee from them?

Much of this is because of humans' moral weakness, but part of it is, as mentioned earlier, due to the subtleties and many voices of Satan. Only by being wary and fully alert to his schemes can people escape.

Yes, learning to know God's voice through his Word, through regular prayer communication with him, by commitment to a Bible-believing church fellowship, and by choosing moral and righteous associations, victory with contentment *can* be achieved.

However, the victor must be fully aware that life is a constant stream of peaks and valleys. Knowing and trusting God is not a guarantee that one will escape trouble, stress, and affliction. But as seen in the Old Testament Book of Job, God allows these circumstances to strengthen us, to open our eyes, to give us empathy, to teach us patience and humility, and to build strong character. Through these experiences, we can become useful teachers and counselors who can effectively minister to those who are hurting and dying all around us.

The bloodline regarding the forty-two generations leading to the birth of Christ Jesus, the Messiah, is recorded in the New Testament Book of Matthew, chapter 1, starting with Abraham and continuing through Joseph and Mary. We see that many who sought after God in the Old Testament were part of this progression. Most were common people; some were controversial, but all were people who wanted their lives to count for God. He honored this faithfulness by making their lives of historical and eternal significance.

The beginning, as touched upon earlier from the Old Testament Book of Genesis, is rephrased in the New Testament Gospel of John, first chapter.

> In the beginning was the Word, and the Word was with God, and the Word was God. He was with God in the beginning. Through him all things were made; without him nothing was made that has been made. In him was life, and that life was the light of men. The light shines in the darkness, but the darkness has not understood it. (John 1:1–5 NIV)

Each of us was born with innocence because the seeds of sin lie dormant in a new child until the world's influences "water" him or her, encouraging those influences to grow. After being exposed to these various stimuli, a child begins to entertain thoughts and feelings of lust, greed, animosity, and selfishness. God did not intend this to be so, but the ruler of the world has so perverted the plans and purposes of God in people's minds that they have rejected the King of Kings and followed a path leading to destruction.

The sweet, fresh life of a newborn child is often carelessly or ignorantly transformed into an adolescent, and eventually an adult, who is filled with a confusing array of lifestyle practices. Dysfunctional adults spawn dysfunctional children, since they consciously and unconsciously model sinful behavior, negative feelings, and moral decadence before them. The Old Testament Books of Kings and Chronicles offer the same patterns, which are sadly replicated today. Where a king's children were exposed to godly parents and grandparents during the crucial years of their youth, they became benevolent and moral leaders upon their ascendancy to the throne. Where this was lacking, just the opposite occurred.

In Isaiah 9, we see the prophetic description of the birth and ascendancy of the King of Kings, who set the ultimate pattern for all in authority to follow.

> For unto us a child is born, to us a son is given, and the government will be on his shoulders. And he will be called Wonderful Counselor, Mighty God, Everlasting Father, Prince of Peace.
>
> Of the increase of his government and peace there will be no end. He will reign on David's throne and over his kingdom, establishing it with justice and righteousness from that time on and forever. The zeal of the Lord Almighty will accomplish this. (Isaiah 9:6–7 NKJV)

Therefore, as we read, discuss, and meditate on the beginning and ongoing progression of life here on earth through scripture, we gain a much clearer understanding of our need for an intimate closeness with the stabilizing influence of the living God. We need a "Wonderful Counselor" who utterly understands our inner hurts and perplexities; a "Mighty God" who has power and authority above all others, while having an intense love and concern for even the least of his creation; an "Everlasting Father" who is consistent and just; and the fellowship and brotherhood of the "Prince of Peace" to increase our faith and establish our hope.

CHAPTER 2

THE WANDERING YEARS

Independence, the desire for adventure, the allure of material wealth and possessions, and the biological time table latent in each man and woman, work together to activate the wanderlust of adulthood. Depending upon the extent and consistency of spiritual and moral influences in a child's home, the length and scope of his or her searching process as an adult will be shaped and focused.

In various biblical passages, we read about those who have "sowed their wild oats," or have run from responsibility for a season. One of the most well-known scriptures pertaining to this is the story of the "prodigal" or lost son in the New Testament Book of Luke, in verse 11 of chapter 15. Here was a young man who had been raised by loving, devoted parents but who chose to seek the pleasures of the world rather than the perceived routine lifestyle of his father's farm. This wandering and spending brought self-serving pleasures and excitement initially, but all too quickly resulted in poverty, sorrow, and guilt. When such temporal pleasures end, our mental "eyes" begin to examine the foundational teachings and practices established during our youth. When they are true, honest, and pure, we understand the guilt and realize our need for repentance. Where they have been false, inconsistent, immoral, and confusing, anger, frustration, and further searching often results. In the case of the lost son, we read that he returned home with sincere repentance and was received with gladness and joy (a parallel to our Heavenly Father receiving us when we sincerely repent). However, the scars of his sin remained in his memories, and the wanton disposal of his inheritance certainly tempered his future endeavors.

Perhaps a child has simply wanted to break out of the traditional roles within his or her family structure by seeking college or vocational training at a distant campus. Possibility, they have desired to see other parts of the country or visit foreign lands. Whatever the goal may be, it has been strongly influenced by the direction, pressures, and intimate relationships formed during their childhood and young adult years.

Some people become hungry for knowledge early in life and use books and other literature to satisfy that hunger. Others find that working with their hands singularly, or in association with others, in the creation of various objects, devices, or machinery brings satisfaction. Unfortunately, a lesser but increasing number of people are unfocused and without regular guidance, intimacy, and reinforced hope, exposing a greater need for moral values, ethical practice, and proper conduct. Thus, our nation grows and proliferates, intermingling the haves with the have-nots, the moral with the corrupt, and harmony with disharmony.

Covetousness, as described in the Bible, has so permeated modern humankind that even the most upright citizen has been affected. Advertising on radio and television, in magazines and newspapers, and on the internet, which we all hear, view, or read, has both subtle and blatantly bold enticements. This visual and mental bombardment succeeds in assisting rationalizations of perceived needs for all kinds of possessions because "we deserve" them. The lack of fiscal responsibility or discipline has sent people down the path of depression and despair. Wanting so much to be like their peers, they throw caution to the winds and become hopelessly entangled in a prison of financial and moral distress. Many of the reasons for broken homes, abused wives and children, divorce, bankruptcy, and even suicide, can be traced to a lack of direction and poor spending habits among those involved. Focused people with hope not only for this life but for eternal life through knowledge of the living God and the saving grace of Jesus Christ, have within them the power to resist this lifestyle of excess, while still enjoying life in the fullest sense.

It is perfectly normal for young men and women to wonder about their future vocations, their ultimate mates, and many other aspects of life. However, by having the plan and purpose of life settled within them, a road to satisfaction and fulfillment can be mapped out effectively. Only a strong knowledge and intimate relationship with the King of Kings can bridge the valleys of despair and overcome the mountains of doubt which stand in the way of receiving such peace and fulfillment.

****

Looking back over my own youth, I can point to many areas where events, temptations, and fears played a large part in shaping my life. My parents' separation and divorce when I was at the tender age of eleven resulted in profound emotional changes which affected every aspect of my life. A child's greatest need during his or her young adult years is the security of loving parents and a stable lifestyle. The youthful energies available during those crucial years can be channeled into learning the foundational elements of living when a happy tranquility is present in the home. Since this was not mine to have and enjoy, the stigma and pain I endured at that time was spent on fanciful dreams about our family being whole and "living happily ever after."

At this time in my young life, my religious experiences included attending church or Sunday school periodically, but no in-depth study of the Bible was attempted, or any special spiritual need was ever made evident to me.

Thus, my mind was open to and sought out much of the base or beggarly elements of life as I entered my teenage years. Girls were only for kissing and playing with primarily as objects of sex, to mentally undress and lust after. Mercifully, the Lord spared me from losing complete control in this area by awakening my conscience regarding right and wrong.

I also started learning as I began to mature that God had made women as *equals* who had every right to be treated with dignity and respect in the same manner as men.

Satan has a diabolical plot in mind regarding teenagers, to push them into sexual affairs which cause deep and painful scars, searing their consciences. But this too is part of the wandering process. How a young man or woman manages this drive and temptation is dependent upon their moral and spiritual foundation. Fortunately for me, the building blocks of morality and genuine love had been laid during my infancy, and worked together with God's unseen hand to lead me through this morass of continual enticement. Although I did not make it through unscathed, my strong conscience made the consequences of such illicit affairs of great concern.

At the time in my youth when I should have been focusing my energies on study habits in school, wholesome sporting activities, or other more profitable concerns, mine were instead narrowed and fragmented. To lie or even steal, if it meant receiving the approval of my peers, was part of this chapter for me. In high school, having a car and a girlfriend, and impressing my friends with fast driving, dirty talk, and drinking parties were the necessary priorities. Stopping long enough for serious thought was not possible since every waking minute was consumed. Having few responsibilities for anything of importance led me into further excesses.

In the state of Montana during the 1950s, the highway speed limit was posted as "reasonable and prudent," so to me and my friends that meant it was wide open. Several of us had large displacement motorcycles in those days, and if a caution sign on a curve read "Slow to 40 mph," we would try to take it at 80 mph. To get greater speed on the straight stretches of highway, we would lay down on the bike, wrap our legs around the back fender, and tuck in one arm. In this way, the 100-mph barrier could be exceeded. Only God's grace prevented our early departure from this life. Everything I wanted to involve myself with in those high school and early college days had to be an adventure, mostly without any practical value.

Although I had come through the agony of a broken home experience, I am sure my life parallels many others regarding the searching, wandering years. However, even after marrying and starting my own family, the searching within me kept its momentum, pushing me on and on. When life should have started bringing meaning and fulfillment, the frustrations remained.

The years drifted by until just a few months before my twenty-eighth birthday, my wife and I repented for our sins and received Jesus Christ into our lives. This joyful experience took place during an altar call in a small church a few miles from our home. It started a process in our lives that continues to this day: a process of learning who we are, why we are here, and the best or most profitable use of our energies.

Even though we began to learn a great deal more about living, we had much more knowledge to receive. But the wandering during those first adult years of our lives was over. Our searching had been concluded and the former frustrations began ebbing away.

****

Is it possible to find peace in this world of constant stress and turmoil, or does each individual or couple have to wander and find his or her or their own way? All of us must leave the safety of the nest at some point in time and follow a path of our own. But we don't have to follow this path blindly, or with fear. We can walk in victory, harmony, and satisfaction, knowing that we are only temporary visitors just passing through. We read in the book of Hebrews, chapter 11 where the great men of faith are discussed, that

> All these people were still living by faith when they died. They did not receive the things promised; they only saw them and welcomed them from a distance. And they admitted that they were aliens and strangers on earth. People who say such things show they are looking for a country of their own. If they had been thinking of the country they had left, they would have had the opportunity to return. Instead, they were longing for a better country—a heavenly one. Therefore, God is not ashamed to be called their God, for he has prepared a city for them. (Hebrews 11:13–16 NIV)

As physical as well as spiritual beings, we have only a brief span of time and limited qualities in this life, but we have an unlimited eternity ahead. Thus, when the wandering period of our lives had been concluded, we begin to sense an urgency to make the remaining years productive and of benefit to our fellow humans.

Unquestionably, God has allowed America to become the racial melting pot of the world. This is a positive, wonderful opportunity for those who have become Christians to work hard at stamping out mistrust and bigotry all around them. Different races bring diverse cultures, and we must honor this individuality, yet not compromise the teaching of the Bible in the process.

We must cultivate an open mind and repent of the former narrowly held dogmas of past generations. God created all human beings equally and loves all equally. If we are sincere in our attitudes, can we continue showing arrogance or disrespect to any of his creation? However, those who come to America purposely to seek freedom and the opportunity to have a better life need also to learn English to become properly assimilated into society and the American way of living. To fail to do so keeps them isolated and prevents them from becoming Americans like the rest of us. Given equal opportunity in education, employment, and the other accepted amenities of life as we know them here in America, members of all immigrant groups can and do excel.

We can learn much from each other when we show brotherly love and put forth the effort to offer true friendship to all our fellow Americans.

To fail to strive for this level of dignity and equality is to miss an important part of God's plan and purpose. Just as we cannot "judge a book by its cover," we should not judge people by their outward appearance, what they wear, how they speak, or by their unique cultures. Rather, we need to extend the hand of genuine fellowship to all. For some who have been historically downtrodden, a much greater effort is needed to establish trust. But when the effort is sincere, consistent, and lasting, progress is made and friendships established. Nevertheless, when people of diverse cultures emigrate to the United States to start new lives yet make every effort to fully retain the culture they left behind, difficulties and hardships are their lots, and they often remain an isolated people. America as we know it is not a country of many small nations, but one nation of diverse nationalities with the goal of bringing its people together on an equal basis for the common good of all.

To fail to make the sacrifices necessary to successfully learn the language and laws of the land, while insisting on keeping intact the trappings and dogmas of a foreign culture, causes much animosity and exclusion—exactly the opposite of equality. This is an area for the present and future leaders of America to thoroughly resolve to assure domestic tranquility throughout this great nation. Isolation breeds anger and rebellion, while common communication gives hope and understanding, as recent world history reveals.

One category of people who have been especially difficult for many of us to discuss or extend any sense of genuine friendship towards are those who have chosen the homosexual lifestyle. (The following thoughts and comments are the author's alone and should not be construed as a presentation resulting from any professional, scientific, or medical analysis.)

In reading case studies pertaining to such individuals, it seems that a substantial number of the people who have chosen this lifestyle were from homes of dysfunctional parents, where they were emotionally and/or physically abused, or severely neglected. Being disoriented regarding "normal" relationships, many such children began seeking intimate same-sex alliances to find the security and love they never previously experienced within their family groups. Certainly, at some point in this process, Satan had a part in the inner restlessness and torment which drives them to seek but never find the peace and satisfaction for which they have hungered. Nevertheless, to brand all homosexuals as "demon possessed," like many Christians do, is not always an accurate assessment.

Some men portray certain effeminate characteristics, while certain women display some masculine qualities.

Often when these tendencies are noticed by others, a subtle categorization and consequent mistreatment can cause such individuals to shy away and become introspective. They may begin wondering why they are "different," thus opening themselves up to Satan's lies.

In discussing the homosexual lifestyle with those who have come out of it by God's grace and mercy, they all seem to agree that they were not born that way. Rather, due to traumatic circumstances occurring as early as three or four years of age, these wrong attributes were implanted.

****

After my older brother decided to move back to Montana to live with my dad and stepmother, I, being three years younger, remained with my mother. We had relocated to another state, where I had enrolled in the eighth grade. My mother was busy working to make ends meet, with school involvement keeping me occupied. However, though my uncles took me hunting and fishing periodically, I was still lonely for a full-time father.

During this period, I met an old man and his son (both now deceased); the son was in his early thirties at that time. They owned a combination barber shop and fishing tackle shop just a couple of blocks from the small apartment in which we lived. I would get my hair cut there and spend a lot of time on other occasions looking at all the new fishing lures and equipment. We struck up a friendship after a while, and the younger man would take me to some nearby lakes and rivers where the fishing was especially good. This was fun, and I enjoyed the opportunities as they came about.

As summer arrived and school was out, I had a lot of time on my hands, as most young people do at that age, so I would stop by the tackle shop every day with a wish list a mile long. On one lazy summer day, the younger man asked me if I would like to go along with him on an overnight business trip to a small town several miles from where we lived. He said that he would be able to show me several good fishing areas as we returned the next day. This sounded exciting to me, so I rushed home to get my mother's permission for the trip. She too thought this would be a fun outing for me and gladly said yes.

The trip to the small city lasted two to three hours, so I just sat looking at the mostly pastoral scenery. However, I became aware of an inordinate number of times my host's fingers touched my knee as I sat there. But since the old car had a floor shift lever upon which he rested his hand, I just moved my legs closer to the door and did not think much more about it.

We finally arrived at our destination and checked in to the motel for the night. There was a double bed and a single rollaway, which I assumed would be mine. The motel attendant soon took the rollaway, leaving the double bed for the both of us. Well, I had slept with my brother many times in the past, so I really was not anticipating any problem. At the age of thirteen, I was extremely naïve about many things, especially anything that had sexual overtones.

After dinner at a nearby restaurant, we returned to the motel and got ready for bed. I stripped down to my tee shirt and underwear and jumped into bed, rolling over with my back to my barber "friend," fully intending to go directly to sleep. He too climbed into bed and moved close to me.

I was already near the edge of the bed with only about five or six inches between it and the wall of the room. When he began to touch and rub my lower back side through my underwear, I became aware of his sexual advances and suddenly became extremely frightened as I attempted to slide into the small space between the bed and the wall. By this time, I was so scared I could not speak and did not know what to expect next. He said something that he thought I was one too, and then left me alone.

Nevertheless, my fright was so intense that I remained in that wedged space totally awake for the remainder of that terrible night.

After arriving back home, I was too embarrassed and scared to tell my mother about what had occurred during the trip, and it was not until many years later that I shared the experience with anyone else.

Although nothing actually *happened* that night, the awful trauma of this experience so affected me that, for the next fifteen to twenty years, any time a man put his arm or hand on my shoulder, the hair on the back of my neck would literally stand out and I would feel a sickly fear envelop me. The Lord has graciously taken this fear away completely now that I have known and walked with him for a number of years. However, because of this episode during my youth, I had a seething hatred for homosexuals, and could not visualize them as anything other than depraved wretches in society. But now, by God's grace, I can see these people as victims needing his love and forgiveness. Although my opinion of their lifestyle remains low and unacceptable, I do have compassion for them as needful human beings who Jesus died for on the cross at Calvary. I also know that because God loves them and wants them to be whole, I can show them his love through me.

****

Since it is not God's desire "that any should perish, but that all should come to repentance," his love for *all* humankind will make "whole" any who will receive his son as Savior and Lord, by "renewing their minds" and making them a "new creation" in Christ Jesus (2 Peter 3:9; 1 Thessalonians 5:23–24; Romans 12:2; 2 Corinthians 5:17 NKJV).

Compassion, sensitivity, and *agape*, or God's kind of love, is what all humankind needs, particularly those who have embraced the homosexual lifestyle. They need to know that others care about them as people who are important and have worth. They also need to understand that a loving God created all humankind to be normal, happy, and contented. But by creating us as free moral beings, he left it up to us to choose right or wrong, good, or bad. When young impressionable minds are subjected to moral depravity for extended periods and genuine love is absent, Satan can get a foothold and a perversion of God's plan is often the result.

We see this clearly expressed in Romans, chapter 1, where a spiritual vacuum opens the door for improper choices and subsequent difficulties. Personally, I would label such continued associations as a progressive desensitization of moral truth to the point that emotions overcome realities, and what is inherently wrong seems to *feel* right.

Thankfully, those who find themselves caught up in this lifestyle can choose to change by asking God to help them, first through sincere repentance, then by discussing their thoughts and frustrations with him in prayer, and finally, through obedience to his Word. Temptations will remain, but God will strengthen discipline and cause a transformation to take place. We, who know God's grace and mercy already, must not be smug or lofty as we encounter such new brothers and sisters, since we too were once spiritually blind sinners and had to repent with equal sincerity and sorrow.

Realizing these truths as Christians, we should no longer hate, despise, ridicule, or judge homosexuals but pray for them, befriend them, and model Christian love before them. Their sin is no worse than that of any other. God is just as able by his Spirit and through his people to help them out of this lifestyle as he would an alcoholic, prostitute, or drug addict. God's love, not the world's twisted version of it, will be the pivotal force that reaches these people. We owe them nothing less. However, lest I am misunderstood as judging either softly or harshly regarding this lifestyle, I defer entirely to the Word of God as illuminated for complete understanding by his Holy Spirit. For I know that this is not a battle in the flesh but a spiritual battle which can only be conquered by the saving grace of Jesus Christ.

When anyone wants help in changing his or her own attitudes or beliefs, the Lord Jesus is always available. Since his love is genuine and can be trusted completely, anyone can ask of him and be assured that he will hear and will answer. Nevertheless, that person must be willing to totally surrender to the Lord, ask in faith (which has been established through scripture), and determine in his or her own heart that the choice is not only correct, but is his or her own. No other man's or woman's convincing arguments can fully achieve this decision for those who have become involved in this or any other sin. Rather, they must admit to themselves and to God first that they are sinners, and secondly, that they need the Savior to rescue them.

Romans, chapter 1, verses 16 to 32, is clear and plain for all to understand. The message is further emphasized in Ephesians 4:17–24 and in 5:17–21, Galatians 5:19–21; 2 Peter 2:10, and 1 Thessalonians 4:7. Such sin can become a "millstone around the neck" unless renounced and brought under the blood of Christ. When this is done with pure motives, "The peace of God which transcends all understanding will guard your hearts and your minds in Christ Jesus" (Philippians 4:6–7 NIV).

The wandering process for many concludes only after a brief period. For others, it may take longer and cover a more complex order of events but can, with God's help, be truly resolved.

However, without the help of a loving God, and the power to be an overcomer by his Holy Spirit, many remain trapped in Satan's death grip which they are not able on their own to break. Always searching for that peace and fulfillment and never enjoying its fruition, they continue their wandering often, unfortunately to their graves.

In conclusion, after considering various foundational and difficult aspects of human existence, it is time for many of us to put an end to our wandering days and move on to higher, more fruitful, and joyfully satisfying areas of living.

CHAPTER 3

ENTERING IN BY GRACE

Now that we have touched upon humankind's beginnings and wandering years, let us look at entering into the fullness of life through God's abundant grace. Once the saving knowledge of Jesus Christ is fully comprehended by the heart-opening power of the Holy Spirit, the old self passes away and the new person emerges.

In 2 Corinthians 5, we read:

> Therefore, if anyone is in Christ, the new creation has come: the old has gone, the new is here! (2 Corinthians 5:17 NIV)

With this in mind, we see a little farther on in 2 Corinthians 6 and 7 that we should

> not be yoked together with unbelievers. For what do righteousness and wickedness have

in common? Or what fellowship can light have with darkness? What harmony is there between Christ and Belial? What does a believer have in common with an unbeliever? What agreement is there between the temple of God and idols? For we are the temple of the living God. As God has said: I will live with them and walk among them, and they will be my people.

Therefore, come out from them and be separate, says the Lord. Touch no unclean thing, and I will receive you. I will be a Father to you, and you will be my sons and daughters, says the Lord Almighty.

Since we have these promises, dear friends, let us purify ourselves from everything that contaminates body and spirit, perfecting holiness out of reverence for God." (2 Corinthians 6:14–7:1 NIV)

Embracing Christianity is not simply adding another activity to our lives. It is instead a total commitment, encompassing every aspect of living. When Christ becomes our Lord, Master, and King, we begin to comprehend our responsibilities. We realize our need to be totally committed to him while letting go of all our personal selfish motivations in favor of pleasing him. However, as mentioned in Chapter 2, humans alone in their own strength cannot achieve this, but must have the help of a higher power in the person of the Holy Spirit.

We read in the Book of Acts that, before Jesus ascended into heaven, he instructed the disciples to pray and wait for what the

Father had promised: that he would send the Comforter, who would empower them to be witnesses to the world. In the second chapter of this book, we are told,

> When the day of Pentecost came, they were all together in one place. Suddenly a sound like the blowing of a violent wind came from heaven and filled the whole house where they were sitting. They saw what seemed to be tongues of fire that separated and came to rest on each of them. *All* of them were filled with the Holy Spirit and began to speak in other tongues, or languages, as the Spirit enabled them. (Acts 2:1–4 NIV)

This was the official entry of the Holy Spirit into the world to take up residence for the eternal benefit of all humankind. He remains the "Helper" for the Christian to this day.

In verse 14 of this same chapter of Acts, we find the fisherman Peter, who had shortly before on three separate occasions denied that he knew Jesus for fear of the Jewish leaders, suddenly able to stand up before a large crowd and preach.

> Those who accepted his message were baptized, and about three thousand were added to their number that day. (Acts 2:41 NIV)

Obviously, for an uneducated, rough old fisherman to speak powerfully, persuasively, and fearlessly, only a relatively few days after not being able to stand up to a small servant girl when Jesus was arrested, meant that something tremendous had taken place within him.

The Holy Spirit had moved the knowledge of Christ's reality from Peter's head to his heart, and empowered him to speak with authority. He now understood the Old Testament prophesy regarding the Messiah, and what the Old Testament prophet Joel had expressed so many years earlier regarding the last days (Acts 2:17–21; Joel 2:28–30).

The faith of Peter and the rest of the disciples had allowed them to pray with such power and conviction that many miraculous events took place as the church grew and prospered.

What is this kind of faith, and can we know its power today? In the book of Hebrews, chapter 11 we see what faith is.

> Now faith is confidence in what we hope for and assurance about what we do not see. (Hebrews 11:1 NIV)

Further, in Romans 10, we see that

> faith comes from hearing the message, and the message is heard through the word about Christ. (Romans 10:17 NIV)

Jesus himself said in the Gospel of John, chapter 14,

> "But the Advocate, the Holy Spirit, whom the Father will send in my name, will teach you all things and remind you of everything I have said to you." (John 14:26 NIV)

This came to fruition for Peter when he was baptized in the Holy Spirit on the Jewish day of Pentecost.

In the New Testament Book of 1 Corinthians, chapter 12, we are given a list of the manifestations of the Holy Spirit for the "blood-washed" believer in Christ. The apostle Paul explains that

> There are different kinds of gifts, but the same spirit distributes them. There are different kinds of service, but the same Lord. There are different kinds of working, but in all of them and in everyone the same God at work. (1 Corinthians 12:4–6 NIV)

He goes on to say in verse 7,

> Now to each one the manifestation of the Spirit is given for the common good. (1 Corinthians 12:7 NIV)

Stopping here for a moment, we see that each believer knows he or she has been baptized or filled with the Holy Spirit when he or she asks him to come in, because the manifestation common to each is the speaking in a language not understood by the mind, but rather by the heart or the subconscious.

If we understood this language, we could control what we say, but bypassing the mind allows our deepest feelings and requests to be made known to God. This is explained more fully in Romans 8.

> We do not know what we ought to pray for, but the Spirit himself intercedes for us through wordless groans. And he who searches our hearts knows the mind of the Spirit, because the Spirit intercedes for the saints in accordance with the will of God. (Romans 8:26–27 NIV)

Returning to 1 Corinthians 12, we can take note that, after the initial manifestation, which is available to every believer, God gives the gifts of the Spirit to individuals he chooses. Therefore, the tongue or language given for private, personal prayer life, is not to be used for the edification of the church, with interpretation following. Rather, we must heed Paul's admonition in verses 29–31 of the same chapter.

> Are all apostles? Are all prophets? Are all teachers? Do all work miracles? Do all have gifts of healing? Do all speak in tongues [for the edification of the church]? Do all interpret? Now eagerly desire the greater gifts. (1 Corinthians 12:7–11 NIV)

Take note that Paul offers this in chapter 14.

> I thank God that I speak in tongues more than all of you. But in the church, I would much rather speak five intelligible words to instruct others then ten thousand words in a tongue. (1 Corinthians 14:18–19 NIV)

This strongly indicates that, with his personal prayer language, he spent a lot of time talking to God privately. However, for those who God gives the gift of tongues for the edification of the church, Paul tells us,

> If anyone speaks in a tongue, two or at most three should speak, one at a time, and someone must interpret. If there is no interpreter, the speaker should keep quiet in

> the church and speak to himself and to God.
> (1 Corinthians 14:27–28 NIV)

This further indicates a separation between the common manifestation and the gift. Additional evidence of the manifestation of the Holy Spirit being received by those believers who ask is found in Acts, chapter 10, verses 44–46.

> Even as Peter was saying these things, the Holy Spirit fell upon *all* who were listening to the message. The Jewish believers who came with Peter were amazed that the gift of the Holy Spirit had been poured out upon the Gentiles, too. And there could be no doubt about it, for they heard them speaking in tongues and praising God. (Acts 10:44–46 NLT)

And in chapter 11, Peter exclaims,

> And since God gave these Gentiles the same gift, he gave us when we believed in the Lord Jesus Christ, who was I to stand in God's way? (Acts 11:17 NLT)

Finally, in 1 Corinthians 13, Paul wonderfully describes what love is, and concludes the chapter by stating that

> Prophecy and speaking in unknown languages and special knowledge will become useless. But love will last forever! Now our knowledge is partial and incomplete, and

> even the gift of prophecy reveals only part of the whole picture! But when the time of perfection comes, these partial things will become useless. When I was a child, I spoke and thought and reasoned as a child. But when I grew up, I put away childish things. Now we see things imperfectly, like puzzling reflections in a mirror, but then we will see everything with perfect clarity. All that I know now is partial and incomplete, but then I will know everything completely, just as God now knows me completely. Three things will last forever—faith, hope, and love—and the greatest of these is love. (1 Corinthians 13:8–13 NLT)

Now if we accept this Scripture as truth, that knowledge has definitely not passed away since people gain more knowledge every day (in both the spiritual as well as scientific and secular realms). Therefore, it would follow that prophecies and speaking in unknown languages or "tongues" are still valid for the Christian today, as many believers would attest. When perfection (Jesus) comes, the imperfect will disappear as these puzzling reflections will no longer be relevant.

It must be remembered too that the gifts of the Holy Spirit must be balanced out by the fruit of the Spirit, which is described in the New Testament Book of Galatians, chapter 5.

> But the Holy Spirit produces this kind of fruit in our lives: love, joy, peace, patience, kindness, goodness, faithfulness, gentleness, and self-control. There is no law against these things.

> Those who belong to Christ Jesus have nailed the passions and desires of their sinful nature to his cross and crucified them there. Since we are living by the Spirit, let us follow the Spirit's leading in every part of our lives. Let us not become conceited, or provoke one another, or be jealous of one another. (Galatians 5:22–26 NLT)

Paul urges us in verses 16 to 18 of this same chapter,

> So, I say, let the Holy Spirit guide your lives. Then you won't be doing what your sinful nature craves. The sinful nature wants to do evil, which is just opposite from what the Holy Spirit wants. And the Spirit gives us desires that are opposite from what the sinful nature desires. These two forces are constantly fighting each other, so you are not free to carry out your good intentions. But when you are directed by the Spirit, you are not under obligation to the law of Moses. (Galatians 5:16–18 NLT)

Those who have been in Christian circles for any length of time have certainly heard, read about, or discussed the Pentecostal or charismatic renewal. Though there have been excesses because of humans, the Bible is truth and provides abundant yet simple directions for the sincere believer to know the Lord Jesus as a close friend, and the Holy Spirit as counselor and guide. This dynamic power comes to the Christian through faith in God's Word, and then by asking him for it. In the Gospel of Luke, the chapter 11, beginning with the verse 9, Jesus exhorts us to

> "Ask and it will be given to you; seek and you will find; knock and the door will be opened to you. For everyone who asks receives; the one who seeks finds; and to the one who knocks, the door will be opened.
>
> Which of you fathers, if your son asks for a fish, will give him a snake instead? Or if he asks for an egg, will give him a scorpion? If you then, though you are evil, know how to give good gifts to your children, how much more will your Father in heaven give the Holy Spirit to those who ask him!" (Luke 11:9–13 NIV)

One further admonition from the scriptures is found in the Book of Ephesians, chapter 5.

> Don't act thoughtlessly, but understand what the Lord wants you to do. Don't be drunk with wine, because that will ruin your life. Instead, be filled with the Holy Spirit. (Ephesians 5:17–18 NLT)

****

As mentioned in Chapter 2, my wife and I sincerely repented, asked God to forgive our sins, and received Jesus as our personal Savior and Lord during our late twenties. Since we had no particular knowledge or prejudices regarding Biblical matters, we simply believed if the Bible said it, it was true, and was true for us.

Therefore, when those who had prayed for us, as we received Christ Jesus, showed us the pattern of believers throughout the New Testament book of Acts, and the details of the Spirit-filled life in 1 Corinthians, Romans, Galatians, and Ephesians, we accepted this by fact and faith. When instructed to also pray to receive the infilling power of the Holy Spirit, we found the above-mentioned scripture in Luke 11 to be true. Now for the first time we could communicate with our Lord in a manner never before known or experienced. We would quickly run out of words to pray in English, but found no limit with our heavenly language.

We had been skeptical of those Christians who would say that God had told them this or that, but now understood that he can and does communicate with us. It is no longer praying as a gesture of desperation, but rather praying with expectations of hearing from heaven through the Bible, or through strong impressions which are confirmed by the Bible and by other believers' testimonies.

It is not my intent, however, to try to persuade anyone regarding his or her need to be empowered by the Holy Spirit—the Bible seems to expound upon this adequately.[1] But I know that our lives have never been the same since we asked the Third Person of the Godhead to fill us, give us power to be overcomers, and produce victory in our lives. We still have our times of difficulty, struggles, and sorrow, but we are never without hope. We now have a track record, established over the many years we have trusted in the Lord, and have the assurance in our hearts that he is always in control—even when our vision is temporarily obscured.

****

---

[1] See Appendix

Entering in by grace also includes an active life in the local church. This does not mean just warming the pews on Sunday, but offering our time and talents to help others. Sunday school teaching, working with youth, construction and maintenance, financial counseling, and visiting the aged, ill, and handicapped, are but a few of the areas of service available.

Balancing this with regular times for devotional studies, both in private and in corporate prayer, and a schedule of quality time with spouses and families, our lives will be exciting, fulfilled, and satisfying, while being pleasing to God our Father and our Lord Jesus Christ.

You might be saying, "Who am I that I could do anything of value or significance that others couldn't do better?" or "I just don't have enough knowledge of the Bible to be able to help anyone." We see in the New Testament Book of James, chapter 1, verses 5–8 that

> If you need wisdom, ask our generous God, and he will give it to you. He will not rebuke you for asking. But when you ask him, be sure that your faith is in God alone. Do not waver, for a person with divided loyalty is as unsettled as a wave on the sea that is blown and tossed by the wind. Such people should not expect to receive anything from the Lord. Their loyalty is divided between God and the world, and they are unstable in everything they do. (James 1:5–8 NLT)

As James further observes in chapter 3,

> But the wisdom from above is first of all pure. It is also peace loving, gentle at all times, and

> willing to yield to others. It is full of mercy and the fruit of good deeds. It shows no favoritism and is always sincere. And those who are peacemakers will plant seeds of peace and reap a harvest of righteousness. (James 3:17–18 NLT)

With these thoughts firmly rooted in our minds, we need only to ask and then step out in faith, trusting God for the answers we seek. Remember: nobody can learn to swim until they get into the water.

Another area of paramount value to the Christian today, as it has always been, is worship and praise. True worship and praise are extremely important, because they are the vehicles set up by God to allow us to enter into his presence.

We cannot demand anything from God. However, as we gain knowledge of his Word and regularly communicate with him as our counselor and friend, we can enter into his presence through worship and praise and ask him with great confidence that his specific *will* be accomplished in us, and in the circumstances affecting us each day.

One of the most vivid encounters with God's presence is in the Old Testament Book of 2 Chronicles, chapter 5, when King Solomon had completed construction of God's temple and gathered the priests, singers, and musicians for the dedication ceremony. We read starting in verse 11:

> The priests then withdrew from the Holy Place. All the priests who were there had consecrated themselves, regardless of their divisions. All the Levites who were musicians—Asaph, Heman, Jeduthun and their sons and relatives—stood on the

east of the altar, dressed in fine linen and playing cymbals, harps and lyres. They were accompanied by 120 priests sounding trumpets. The trumpeters and musicians joined in unison, to give praise and thanks to the Lord.

Accompanied by trumpets, cymbals and other instruments, they raised their voices in praise to the Lord and sang:

"He is good; his love endures forever."

Then the temple of the Lord was filled with the cloud, and the priests could not perform their service because of the cloud, for the glory of the Lord filled the temple of God. (2 Chronicles 5:11–14 NIV)

Oh, how America, as well as the other nations of the world, need to heed this message today.

Therefore, entering into God's presence, through sincere worship and praise, is necessary if we are to experience all the blessings God has in store for us. Without this *entering in* we have only "a form of Godliness but are denying its power" (2 Timothy 3:5 NIV).

When we think of the whole world as either evangelized or unevangelized, we can begin to understand our major role as Christians. Jesus paid the supreme price of his life for all humankind, and gave us his salvation so that we could be his arms, legs, and voice in carrying the Gospel message to those who have not heard. In America and other mostly western nations where the Gospel of Christ has been openly preached and clearly made known, men and women have the choice to either accept or reject the Savior.

However, in many other nations of the world, where Christianity is not allowed, the people of course do not have these choices. The Bible's clear mandate is for all people everywhere to have the Gospel presented to them in their own language so that all will have the opportunity to know God's love.

In the prophetic book of Revelation 7:9, the apostle John writes,

> After this I looked and there before me was a great multitude that no one could count, from *every* nation, tribe, people and language, standing in front of the throne and before the lamb. (Revelation 7:9 NIV)

How can this prophesy be fulfilled unless we as God's people obey the great commission? In Mark 16, Jesus exhorts us to

> "Go into all the world and preach the good news to everyone everywhere." (Mark 16:15 NLT)

When this mandate has been completed, there will be nothing to prevent the Lord's return for his church. Since each one of us who call ourselves Christians is the church, we are to accept the challenge and embrace this as our personal vision or commitment to sacrificially do our part.

Being baptized in the Holy Spirit gives us power to be witnesses, as explained in Acts 1.

> But you will receive power when the Holy Spirit comes on you; and you will be my witnesses in Jerusalem (your city and mine),

and in all Judea (your state and mine) and Samaria (your country and my country), and to the ends of the earth (which of course, means the rest of the world). (Acts 1:8 NIV)

In the King James Version of the Bible, and also in the original Greek, the verse includes the word *both* just before the four locations mentioned, meaning the work is to be done simultaneously and not progressively.

Since God's amazing grace is always sufficient to meet every area of human needs, we are extremely blessed people. When we truly know him, have the assurance of his salvation and eternal life, have been empowered by his Spirit, are actively involved in his service, are meeting the needs of our families, and are strongly supporting missions with our prayers, time, and finances, we can know that we are truly *entering in by grace*.

CHAPTER 4

PROCEEDING ONWARD IN FAITH

"Now faith is confidence of what we hope for and assurance about what we do not see" (Hebrews 11:1 NIV). Although we touched on this somewhat in Chapter 3, growing in faith is a continuing process throughout the Christian's life.

New Christians usually possess a lot of zeal and considerable faith, but generally lack the depth in their convictions to be consistent soul-winners. This takes a period of time, since each new believer needs to be discipled by mature Christians so as to become grounded and established in Bible doctrine, and thereby grow in faith. Certainly, for these people to gain trust in us, we must spend time getting to know them. This is especially true for the new believer, since the initial euphoria of the born-again experience soon wanes if not kept alive by learning how to talk to and with the Lord. Therefore, becoming an active participant in a strong Bible-based local church, coming under the spiritual authority of pastoral leadership, and openly receiving regular fellowship and teaching, completes these beginning processes.

The writer of Hebrews, in chapter 5 starting with verse 12, exhorts us about spiritual immaturity and the need to continue growing in our faith.

> For though by this time you ought to be teachers, you need someone to teach you again the first principles of the oracles of God; and you have come to need milk and not solid food. For everyone who partakes only of milk is unskilled in the word of righteousness, for he is a babe. But solid food belongs to those who are of full age, that is, those *who by reason of use* have their senses exercised to discern both good and evil. (Hebrews 5:12 NKJV; emphasis added)

He continues in Hebrews, chapter 6 by outlining "the peril of not progressing."

> Therefore, leaving the discussion of the elementary *principles* of Christ, let us go on to perfection, not laying again the foundation of repentance from dead works and of faith toward God, of the doctrine of baptisms, of laying on of hands, or resurrection of the dead, and of eternal judgements. And this we will do if God permits. (Hebrews 6:1–2 NKJV)

As we learn together and grow stronger, *by reason of use*, God will help us learn to witness more effectively and find exceeding great joy in the process.

It should be understood that God allows much in the way of trials, sorrows, and stress to enter our lives in the years following our conversion, to mold us into the people he desires us to be. We must grow spiritually strong so we don't

> become weary in doing good, for at the proper time we will reap a harvest if we do not give up. Therefore, as we have opportunity, let us do good to all people, especially to those who belong to the family of believers. (Galatians 6:9–10 NIV)

Through all of our positive and negative experiences, however, we can trust in and rely upon God to be faithful. In the Old Testament Book of Isaiah, chapter 55, beginning with verse 6, we read:

> Seek the Lord while he may be found;
> Call on him while he is near.
> Let the wicked forsake his way
> and the unrighteous their thoughts.
> Let him turn to the Lord, and he will have mercy on them,
> and to our God, for he will freely pardon.
> "For my thoughts are not your thoughts,
> Neither are your ways my ways," declares the Lord." (Isaiah 55:6–8 NIV)

As new Christians, we somehow believe we need to tell God how he should accomplish something we have asked of him. However, since God sees the beginning and end of matters, his answer, or means of accomplishing our prayer requests, may be a whole lot different than what we expected. Many times, his answer is simply no, because he has a different timetable than ours, or he may want us to learn some valuable lesson first.

In the New Testament Book of James, chapter 2, verses 14–26, we find that faith alone is not good enough.

> What good is it, my brothers, if a man claims to have faith but has no deeds? Can such faith save them? Suppose a brother or sister is without clothes and daily food.
>
> If one of you says to him, "Go, I wish you well; keep warm and well fed," but does nothing about his physical needs, what good is it? In the same way, faith by itself, if not accomplished by action, is dead.
>
> But someone will say, "You have faith; I have deeds. Show me your faith without deeds, and I will show you my faith by my deeds." You believe there is one God? Good! Even the demons believe that—and shudder.
>
> You foolish person, do you want evidence that faith without deeds is useless? Was not our ancestor Abraham considered righteous for what he did when he offered his son Isaac on the Altar? You see that his faith and his actions were working together, and his faith was made complete by what he did. And the scripture was fulfilled that says, "Abraham believed God, and it was credited to him as righteousness," and he was called God's friend. You see that a person is considered righteous by what they do and not by faith alone.

> In the same way, was not even Rahab the prostitute considered righteous for what she did when she gave lodging to the spies and sent them off in a different direction? As the body without the spirit is dead, so faith without deeds is dead. (James 2:14–26 NIV)

What we can readily see is that to become strong, effective Christians, we need to become active in being of service to others. The apostle Paul tells us in his letter to the Romans, chapter 12,

> Just as each of us has one body with many members, and these members do not all have the same function, so in Christ we who are many, form one body, and each member belongs to all the others. We have different gifts, according to the grace given us. If your gift is prophesying, then prophesy in accordance to your faith. If it is serving, then serve; if it is teaching, then teach; if it is to encourage, then give encouragement; if it is giving, then give generously; if it is to lead, then do it diligently; if it is showing mercy, do it cheerfully. (Romans 12:4–8 NIV)

It is well for all Christians to build upon their God-given strengths and talents, rather than wishing to be or trying to be like others.

When everyone does what he or she does best for the good of the body of Christ, then all tasks are accomplished in a timely and satisfactory manner. The flip side of this is when many do not perform their parts of the body function, requiring the remaining few to function in areas where they may not have the talent or gifting. This is one reason why many churches today are weak. A lot of people don't want to become involved or obligated, and really expect their pastors and paid staff to bring everything together. This kind of response is not only to our shame, but when we fail to do our part, we also lose a great deal of joy and satisfaction for ourselves and are not pleasing to God. His love is unconditional, but his marvelous gift of salvation was given so that we could be fruitful for his kingdom and bring him honor and glory in willing service for him. We must remember that God created each of us as a unique individual with specific talents to fulfill a special purpose in his kingdom.

Paul exhorts us in the book of Ephesians to be strong and equipped for combat against the devil. In chapter 6, starting with verse 10, we are told,

> Finally, be strong in the Lord and in his mighty power. Put on the full armor of God so that you can take your stand against the devil's schemes. For our struggle is not against flesh and blood, but against the rulers, against the authorities, against the powers of this dark world and against the spiritual forces of evil in heavenly realms.
>
> Therefore, put on the full armor of God, so that when the day of evil comes, you may be able to stand your ground, and after you have done everything, to stand. Stand firm then, with the belt of truth buckled around your waist, with the breastplate of righteousness in place, and with your feet fitted with the readiness that comes from the Gospel of peace. In addition to all this, take up the shield of faith, with which you can extinguish

all the flaming arrows of the evil one. Take the helmet of salvation and the sword of the Spirit, which is the word of God. And pray in the Spirit on all occasions with all kinds of prayers and requests. With this in mind, be alert and always keep on praying for all the Lord's people. (Ephesians 6:10–18 NIV)

****

Since coming to know the Lord in early 1963, my wife and I have experienced all types of temptations, known financial struggles, tasted the bitterness of depression, and realized the futility of anger. But most importantly, these events and conditions proved to have been for our ultimate good as we look back over the years. Through them all, God was faithful!

The apostle Paul tells us in 1 Corinthians, chapter 10,

> So, if you think you are standing firm, be careful that you don't fall! No temptation has seized you except what is common to man. And God is faithful; he will not let you be tempted beyond what you can bear.
>
> But when you are tempted, he will also provide a way out so that you can endure it. (1 Corinthians 10:12–13 NIV)

We gradually learned that we did not have to give in to every pressure that came our way. With God's help, we could say no or make a rational decision to walk away from these which would have an adverse effect on us. We no longer operated only by impulse, but started learning the strength of patience.

By placing our faith and trust in God to help us, we began to witness a wonderful transformation in our outlook on life and our relationship with each other. People became more important than things, which translated into a peace and contentment not previously comprehended.

We have had numerous opportunities to apply and strengthen our faith through sharing of the Gospel message with those who the Holy Spirit had prepared. One incident in particular involved the elderly father of a good friend of ours. He had been taken to the hospital and not given much time to live. After talking with our friend about the situation, I felt strongly impressed to go visit this man, who I had never before met. Our friend's mother, who we knew casually, was in the hospital room when I arrived. She said I should talk to him alone, and quickly excused herself from the room. For the next several minutes we talked and determined that he was desirous of hearing the scriptures on salvation, which we proceeded to cover.

He seemed especially alert, and when I asked him if he would like to pray to receive Jesus into his heart, he quickly said yes. We prayed a simple prayer of repentance and acceptance together. I then asked him if he sensed that the Lord had come in. He paused for a moment and then said in his Swedish accent, "Yah, he did!"

The sheer joy of seeing this old man being transformed at the eleventh hour of his life was such an emotional high for me that I had to stop my car on the way home from the hospital because the tears were flowing so profusely my vision was obscured. Just two days later, he died but he left this life for a much better one because the Holy Spirit had prepared his heart and he was heaven bound.

What I learned is when God impresses us to be of service for him, we should never stop to examine our own perceived deficiencies, lack of knowledge, or limited talents, but rather walk in faith in the belief that whatever we lack he will provide. In this way he receives all the glory and we receive great satisfaction and joy while all the time knowing that

> God chose the foolish things of the world to shame the wise; God chose the weak things of the world to shame the strong. He chose the lowly things of this world and the despised things—and the things that are not—to nullify the things that are, so that no one may boast before him.
>
> It is because of him that you are in Christ Jesus, who has become for us wisdom from God—that is, our righteousness, holiness and redemption. Therefore, as it is written: "Let him who boasts boast in the Lord." (1 Corinthians 1:27–31 NIV)

****

In the Old Testament Book of Malachi, chapter 3, beginning with verse 8, we read:

> Should people cheat God? Yet you have cheated me! But you ask, "What do you mean? When did we ever cheat you?" You have cheated me of the tithes and offerings due to me. You are under a curse, for your whole nation has been cheating me. Bring all the tithes into the storehouse so there will be enough food in my Temple. If you do, says the Lord Almighty, I will open the windows of heaven for you. I will pour out a blessing so great you won't have enough room to take it in! Try it! Let me prove

it to you! Your crops will be abundant, for I will guard them from insects and disease. Your grapes will not shrivel before they are ripe, says the Lord Almighty. Then all the nations will call you blessed, for your land will be such a delight, says the Lord Almighty. (Malachi 3:8–12 NLT)

One of the most difficult areas to allow faith to take hold for the new believer is the giving of his or her income to the work of the Lord. To serve others, to help with the needed work, and to share the Good News seems to be easiest to master for them. However, the giving of hard-earned resources is often met with a great deal of stress. This is where faith is tested and strengthened. One of their first thoughts is, *I can spend my money more wisely than the church board of elders and deacons can,* or *my financial commitments are just too tight to allow giving a full tithe of my income.* But it has to be a matter of faith to give sacrificially, as suggested in the above verses from Malachi.

It is amazing, but a faithful person can't out-give God. Once the giving barrier is broken, the money left over is always sufficient to meet or exceed anticipated needs. Otherwise, in most cases the unpaid tithe or offering is dissipated by unexpected doctor bills, automobile breakdowns and repairs, plus numerous other unanticipated expenses. When a person is obedient to God through faith, the Lord's often unseen blessings fulfill and satisfy even beyond expectations, and his work on earth continues unhindered. Yes, people will spend the monies we give, but when we give them to God by faith, they are accepted by him and credited to our heavenly bank account.

Thus, as we grow and mature by experiencing many of life's joys, sorrows, and spiritual battles, we find as we look back over the peaks and valleys of our journey, we are definitely believers who have been *proceeding onward in faith*.

Chapter 5

GAINING STRENGTH WITHIN GOD'S CALLING

God's plan and purpose for each of us is not to make us religious fanatics, nor does he want everyone who receives him as Lord and Savior to become pastors or evangelists. What he does want, however, is for each of us to mature and excel with the talents he has given us. As we study and work hard at our professions, whatever they may be, he will open doors of opportunity for successful living, and bring about spiritual encounters for sharing the Gospel. The apostle Paul tells us in 1 Corinthians, chapter 7,

> Brothers and sisters, each person, as responsible to God, should remain in the situation they were in when God called them. (1 Corinthians 7:24 NIV)

If we are businesspeople, we should work hard to be the best we can be, with honesty, integrity, and compassion as our goals.

At the same time, we need to become diligent in our spiritual commitment to Bible study and prayer, so that our faith and knowledge will be strengthened and a healthy humility will enter in. If, on the other hand, God calls us to be full-time pastors or evangelists, we can be assured he will prepare us for such service with wisdom, sensitivity, and clear direction.

Some people seem to have a tough time trying to find just where they fit in the workforce. Consequently, they move from one job to another. Such people need to take time to discuss this in detail with the Lord, asking him to give them insight and discernment regarding their special talents or giftings. Then, as these become known to them, they should begin to seek out the career paths in which they have a more natural fit.

Our knowledge should also begin to include an understanding of taxes and legal matters, social and political issues, and the necessary steps to provide safety and security for those who are our responsibility. Obviously, as adults we want to make mature judgments regarding the many and varied factors facing us each day. None of us really has the time to be as immature and irresponsible as we once were, but with God's help and sobering presence, we can all embrace success.

For those who find they are locked in a job that is difficult and unfulfilling, such shackles can be broken. However, this will take patience, discipline, and walking by faith as new doors are opened. God, our Heavenly Father, wants each of his offspring to prosper and enjoy happiness. Therefore, through Christ's salvation, together with the indwelling Holy Spirit, he has imparted to each believer the power and capability for success.

By applying the knowledge and truth of God's Word to our everyday walk, we soon find that we do indeed receive genuine encouragement and gain greater strength.

"If there is a will, there is a way" is an expression that carries a whole lot of truth. When we determine in our hearts to seek better education or more in-depth training to improve our skills and abilities, there will be definite sacrifices of time, effort, and finances involving ourselves and our families. Nevertheless, the ultimate gain will far outweigh this initial price while expanding our potential. It can also be a time for the family to pull together in a united effort, opening greater communications and establishing bold patterns for younger members to eventually emulate as similar needs arise for them.

****

Back when I was finishing high school, I lacked any real sense of direction regarding future occupations, and fantasized about being this or that without any idea whether I possessed any abilities in such areas. But I did know that without some training or college preparation, my future was cloudy at best.

My father wanted me to attend and complete college since he had not been able to when he was my age. Therefore, I enrolled in a junior college my first year, in part to please him. After this initial year was over and I found that my study habits from high school were woefully inadequate for college courses, I came to a crossroad. Either I buckled down and worked a lot harder, or quit and tried something else. The U.S. Navy and Korean War G.I. Bill of Rights for such veterans became my answer.

In some ways, I could say that initially, military service was just marking time. Yet it did help me to grow up and learn to make more mature judgments. During my Navy tenure, I learned the barbering trade and became proficient before being discharged. Although this work was challenging and enjoyable, I had now been married for a while and would soon have a second child to care for. At that time, unless you owned your own shop, making a living for a growing family in the barbering trade was just not possible. Realizing this, I became determined to continue with college to earn at least a bachelor's degree, and then find a position somewhere in industry. Not knowing initially which major to follow, I enrolled in a lot of courses that were unnecessary, but kept pushing on with no thought of giving up until a specific major came into focus.

Graduation day came and with it several job interviews. I began to realize that this long-sought degree did indeed open doors that most assuredly would have been closed without it.

Many years, and a whole lot of experiences, have now passed by, but the extra hardships absorbed by my family and me to gain a formal education were well worth every effort and every sacrifice.

My whole purpose for relating this is to encourage anyone and everyone to refuse to give up or become impatient. Rather, people should always keep their eyes on the goals (even if not completely understood) and not allow pressures to detour them. We must be fully aware that God's timing is consistent and appropriate for us, even when we have other ideas.

****

If we are in right standing with God and our fellow humans, and are trusting in his Word, we can by faith trust him to bring about the best for us even if it happens weeks, months, or years later. Maturity with stability takes time, and often involves considerable pain, so we must learn to yield to his judgments and not just our own.

We are told in Hebrews, chapter 10,

> So do not throw away your confidence; it will be richly rewarded. You need to persevere so that when you have done the will of God, you will receive what he has promised. (Hebrews 10:35–36 NIV)

We can also see in the Bible that those who were successful and used by God to carry forth the gospel had spent the time necessary to master a trade. The apostle Paul was a tentmaker (Acts 18:3); Peter was a commercial fisherman; Luke was a medical doctor; and of course, Jesus was trained as a carpenter from his youth.

Although it is possible to just fall into an occupation which provides all the right ingredients for contentment and financial reward, purposeful planning with a person's own obvious skills and talents in mind will have a much higher level of real success and yield the greatest satisfaction.

To bring this all together then, each man and woman must earnestly desire and work diligently at learning where his or her skills lie, then apply the necessary effort despite the cost to gain the knowledge required to achieve the goal. For the Christian, who repeatedly calls on God for wisdom and strength, this can be more easily realized.

After focusing in on those areas where we believe God has gifted us, we should put forth every effort to explore the opportunities presented, while not allowing ourselves to lose hope by negative feedback of peers, friends, or relatives. The many years spent in gainful employment can therefore be enjoyable and much less stressful when we diligently pursue that inner knowledge implanted by God.

Finding an excellent job with a reputable company or organization is of course what most young men and women strive for after completing college or vocational training. However, it is interesting to note that a majority of those who came to America as immigrants from Asian countries came looking to start businesses of their own.

They may take jobs first, but as soon as financially feasible, they become self-employed businesspeople. By formulating a good business plan, accepting considerable risk together with extensive work hours, most are eventually able to gather considerable wealth. Of course, those who succeed have had to also master the administrative skills necessary to operate a successful company, however small it may be initially.

By much self-sacrifice and significant effort, many individuals or couples have turned their vision for businesses of their own into realities. Therefore, as James 1 tells us,

> If you need wisdom, ask our generous God, and he will give it to you. He will not rebuke you for asking. (James 1:5 NLT)

Therefore, ask God for wisdom and guidance if you feel shackled in an unfulfilling employment situation. Success in a business of your own could be the answer to the self-satisfaction and financial freedom you have desired, while also allowing you to bless God with your abundance.

It should be remembered that, as believers, we must diligently strive to attain balance between employment demands, family, and personal desires. Too much work pressure damages family relationships and too many personal pleasures lead to selfish initiatives that often alienate those we love.

By presenting our perceived needs to God in prayer as a family, and seeking his grace as we proceed forward in faith, our activities can be fulfilling and wonderfully inclusive, while we *gain strength within God's calling.*

Chapter 6

ENCOURAGEMENT, COUNSELLING, AND DISCIPLESHIP

Now, as mature believers in Jesus Christ, and knowing the power of the Holy Spirit in our lives, we need to become actively involved in God's family so that our talents may be more fully and specifically utilized.

As we observe the strengths and weaknesses of our spiritual brothers and sisters, our own strengths and weaknesses will become better known. Certainly, we have discovered how much we need this greater family, for encouragement, counseling, and for adding further vitality to the overall discipling process we are continually undergoing.

In the Book of 1 Corinthians, chapter 16, we see that the apostle Paul exhorts us to

> Be on guard; stand firm in the faith; be courageous. Be strong. And do everything with love. (1 Corinthians 16:13–14 NLT)

Again, in chapter 14, verse 20 of the same book, he tells us,

> Brothers and sisters, stop thinking like children. In regard to evil be infants, but in your thinking be adults. (1 Corinthians 14:20 NIV)

Since we who believe realize that we were released from the bondage of our sinful habits by Christ's shed blood, we see in Galatians, chapter 5 that

> It is for this freedom that Christ set us free. Stand firm then, and do not let yourselves be burdened again by a yoke of slavery. (Galatians 5:1 NIV)

Further confirmation of our plans and purpose is offered in Philippians, chapter 1:

> Whatever happens, conduct yourselves in a manner worthy of the Gospel of Christ. Then whether I come and see you or only hear about you in my absence, I will know that you stand firm in one spirit, striving together as one for the faith of the Gospel without being frightened in any way by those who oppose you. (Philippians 1:27–28 NIV)

And finally in chapter 2 of this book, verses 1–4, Paul concludes,

> Therefore, if you have an encouragement from being united with Christ, if any comfort from his love, if any common sharing in the Spirit, if any tenderness and compassion, then make my joy complete by being like-minded, having the same love, being in one spirit and of one mind.
>
> Do nothing out of selfish ambition or vain conceit. Rather in humility value others above yourselves, not looking to your own interests but each of you to the interests of others. (Philippians 2:1–4 NIV)

Lastly, in Philippians, chapter 4, Paul exhorts us with these words.

> Finally, brothers and sisters, whatever is true, whatever is noble, whatever is right, whatever is pure, whatever is lovely, whatever is admirable—if anything is excellent or praiseworthy—think about such things. Whatever you have learned or received or heard from me, or seen in me—put into practice. And the God of peace will be with you. (Philippians 4:8–9 NIV)

****

When my wife and I first came to know the Lord Jesus as Savior, we were like new babies and needed our mature Christian friends as spiritual fathers, mothers, brothers, and sisters. We just could not seem to get enough fellowship, because it was so new and wonderful. Just like physical babies need constant attention at first, spiritual babies are no different. In fact, spiritual babies have the added burden of fighting off the lies of the devil. We were no exceptions to this but were surrounded with strong believers from the beginning who helped us become grounded in the Word and in faith. After about a year of this learning process, God saw fit to move us to a new area in another state, many miles away from these newly found family members. Thus, we had graduated to become counselors and disciplers of other new Christians.

Had this not occurred when it did, our spiritual growth might have been inhibited, and our opportunity to be blessings to others could have been detoured.

We were forced to walk by faith after this move, and found that God's Holy Spirit and abundant grace truly became our sufficiency as we did. The Lord gave us the joy of leading several to him, and the chance to pray with and for many others as we grew steadily stronger in him. We quickly began to understand that the more we gave of ourselves for the benefit of others, the more the Lord blessed and encouraged us.

One of the highlights of this time after our move was that I had the privilege of praying with the chaplain of the state prison, with two other brothers (who were pastors), for the baptism of the Holy Spirit. This was in the chaplain's own office, and he was wonderfully filled, which enhanced his ministry afterwards.

We learned that we had to move beyond thinking of doing good to stepping out in faith and doing it. When we had followed through on this after prayer, we were never disappointed in the outcome.

****

When someone we know comes to the Lord, repents, and receives him as Savior, or we have the joy of leading a total stranger to him, we must realize that our spiritual parenting has only just begun.

This new born babe in Christ needs to lean heavily on the mature Christians around him or her to gain spiritual strength and vitality. Without such fellowship and shared Bible study with the members of the body of Christ, discouragement and frustration often plague the new believer, and opens him or her up to the lying schemes of Satan.

It is vital that we introduce the new believer to other, more mature Christians, especially if we are not able to spend the needed time to disciple them ourselves. We help them to be comfortable as they enter the new life, they have received from the Lord by inviting them for fellowship at every opportunity presented. As we know from our own experience, new believers have an insatiable appetite for God's Word and will make themselves available when a friend is involved with them.

Many of us have plenty of advice to offer others, even when we are carrying around a load of our own problems. When we find ourselves doing this, we are not being helpful counselors and need to spend some time on our face before God in prayer. The Lord Jesus himself tells us in both Matthew, chapter 7 and Luke, chapter 6, that "we need to get the plank out of our own eye before we point out the speck of sawdust in our brother's eye" (Mathew 7:3–5 and Luke 6:41 NIV).

In other words, when a Christian brother or sister comes to us for advice or counsel, we are being hypocrites if we offer answers or solutions when we ourselves are experiencing similar problems.

It is far better to admit up front that we do not have an answer or solution, than to allow pride to puff us up. The Bible indicates in many areas that God hates prideful hearts but loves those who are humble. However, what we *can* do is pray for each other that God will provide the help and answers we need.

Certainly, all of us who have walked with the Lord for many years have gone through experiences where we were refined by fire and sifted as wheat. How we reacted to these experiences has established a portfolio of knowledge to share with others who are new in their spiritual walk. However, when these new believers confide in us and seek answers to many perplexing problems, we must be diligent to keep these expressions confidential and share them only with God. Our counseling efforts should be based on scriptural foundations which were instilled in our own hearts as we encountered similar difficulties in the past. In this manner, God, through the Holy Spirit, can minister to them using us as his channels.

Obviously, God has gifted some believers with discernment and wisdom beyond what others can offer.

When situational problems are shared by the new believer that are beyond our experiences or abilities, we should always refer the person to a pastor or professional Christian counselor for further resolution.

Now, having had our talents and skills used by God for the benefit of others, it is time to consider the *priorities that remain*.

Chapter 7

THE PRIORITIES THAT REMAIN

The realization of what the father and the son gave and sacrificed for each one of us should have by now fully reached well within the realm of comprehension our finite minds are able to grasp. In other words, the plan and purpose for God's gift of salvation might be fully implemented in and through us, his people. Eternal life is certainly his promise and our hope; but more than that, his loving touch and presence in our lives has encouraged and continues to encourage our training and preparation for effective Christian service.

Have we read our lessons and studied them well? Has our on-the-job training been thorough and complete? Are we prepared to take an active part in his army, the body of Christ? His salvation opened the door for us, his Holy Spirit has thoroughly equipped us, and we have now become aware of our own innate talents. Therefore, the priorities we now recognize encompass the reality of eternity with our loving God in the inexplicable brilliance of heaven, and the contrasting, unimaginable torment, darkness, and eternal separation from God in hell.

No matter how much we may have gained in material wealth, possessions, and knowledge during our lives, only what we learned and accomplished for eternity will be credited to our spiritual bank account. We read in Romans, chapter 10:

> How then, can they call on the one they have not believed in? And how can they believe in the one of whom they have not heard? And how can they hear without someone preaching to them? And how can they preach unless they are sent? As it is written: "How beautiful are the feet of those who bring good news!" (Romans 10:14–15 NIV)

We may not have received calls from God to be pastors, teachers, or evangelists, but we can gladly give out the good news when the Holy Spirit opens the door for us to do so. It is not something we must do out of obligation or duty, but rather because of God's love in us and for the sheer joy of being used in his service. Just knowing that so many people all around will never know about or see heaven should spur us on. Thankfully, because God so loved the world (as we learned from the familiar passage in John 3:16) he desires that all peoples share in eternal life. We, being his arms, legs, and mouthpiece, are the means he uses to spread the gospel to those around us. He prepares the soil of their hearts by his Holy Spirit, but we must plant the good seed and provide the nourishment needed to assure a bountiful harvest.

Therefore, to be effective soldiers in God's army, we must schedule time to sit in his presence, time to fellowship with his people, and time to give account of his grace with love and purpose.

This is a high priority, but must not come at the expense of our spouses and families.

They should be included as team players with us whenever possible to support the effort with prayer, and freely participate as the skills of effective witnessing are practiced and learned—as Hebrews 5:14 told us earlier *"by constant use."*

Though the Bible declares that we are to occupy until the Lord comes back for us, we are not to become imbalanced in our thinking. Since no one has been told the time of his return, we should live this life as if we were going to live to a ripe old age while keeping in mind the possibility that he might return today or tomorrow.

A mature Christian is a disciple of Christ, or a disciplined one, and therefore, has the power of the Holy Spirit within to plan and prepare for the future when his or her days of gainful employment are over. This is another priority that should not be overlooked or underestimated. The present generation is a "now" group of people who tend to put themselves desperately in debt to have the pleasures and playthings of the world immediately. This has short-circuited many plans for fiscal responsibility during the peak earning years, and has placed a terrible burden on our society.

With Christian discipline to give purpose to our thoughts and actions, we can overcome the pressures of the world and maintain financial equilibrium, thereby freeing us to be of greater service to our Lord during retirement.

When we grasp a full understanding of this early on in our Christian walk, we begin to find that God's rich blessings more than make up for any of the temporal pleasures we may have given up along life's way. We read in Mark, chapter 8:

> What good is it for someone to gain the whole world, yet forfeit his soul? (Mark 8:36 NIV)

And, Psalms, chapter 37 says,

> The Lord makes firm the steps of the one who delights in him; though he may stumble, he will not fall, for the Lord upholds him with his hand. I was young and now I am old, yet I have never seen the righteous forsaken or their children begging bread. They are always generous and lend freely; their children will be a blessing. Turn from evil and do good; then you will dwell in the land forever. For the Lord loves the just and will not forsake his faithful ones. (Psalms 37:23–28 NIV)

The Life Application Study Bible, New Living Translation, by Tyndale House Publishers, offers a helpful evaluation chart as an addendum to the fifth chapter of Hebrews, showing the choices Christians make and the ways those choices change with personal growth. These are as follows.

Mature Choices	**Versus**	**Immature Choices**
Teaching others	rather than	just being taught
Developing depths of understanding	rather than	struggling with the basics
Self-evaluation	rather than	self-criticism
Seeking unity	rather than	promoting disunity

Desiring spiritual challenges	rather than	desiring entertainment
Careful study and observation	rather than	opinions and half-hearted efforts
Active faith	rather than	cautious apathy and doubt
Confidence	rather than	fear
Feelings and experiences Evaluated in the light of God's Word	rather than	experiences evaluated according to feelings

****

It certainly did not come overnight, but by exposure with other mature Christians, Bible study, and by witnessing and sharing the gospel message, my wife and I have had the privilege and joy of leading numerous people onto salvation and the baptism of the Holy Spirit. Not being trapped by the obligations of the world has set us free to follow these greater opportunities with peace in our hearts.

We both know and are fully aware that some believers have difficulties in witnessing, even though they love the Lord and are versed in scripture. We cannot all be like a Paul or Timothy of the New Testament. But we can still be God's witnesses by our actions, and by our willingness to help in the building up of the body of believers with the skills and talents we do possess.

Therefore, when witnessing opportunities are presented, we have found that God always helps us when we, by faith, take the first step.

※※

Many people who were shy and fearful of speaking out in a group have been stretched during their Christian walk. Experience does provide strength, stability, and confidence. Experience is what life becomes—ongoing and ever increasing as the years pass by. Should such experience remain locked up within us, or can we pass it on as a source of energy and encouragement for others?

We do not have to (and should not) give advice unless it is asked for, but we can offer things to consider to help others reach proper conclusions to unanswered questions they may be pondering. Without reaching deep into our lifetime experiences, many of us become only parrots for the experiences of others, which may or may not be valid. Therefore, *the priorities that remain* are crucial, but are of such a nature that they will progressively bring much happiness and fulfillment into our lives as we yield to the gentle urgings of the Holy Spirit of God.

Chapter 8

THE HOME STRETCH IN SIGHT

As we have apprehended God's sure calling in our lives, have diligently worked at fulfillment, and have been careful to impart the knowledge we have gained to others, we can be assured that our efforts have produced eternal benefits, pleasing our Heavenly Father. However, the challenges presented to us have not yet been completed, nor is our work totally fulfilled—but *the home stretch is in sight.*

The years of studying God's Word, sitting under the teaching, and preaching of anointed speakers, and numerous hours praying have produced good fruit in us for the benefit of those just beginning the journey.

We are never washed up, phased out, or obsolete if we continue to lovingly encourage and spiritually support our Christian brothers and sisters. Strength and consistency in the faith have prepared us to be examples to those who are traveling earlier, more perplexing sections of their spiritual walk. By God's abundant and amazing grace, he brought us through life's temptations, disappointments, and difficulties to the place where our worship and praise unto him is genuine and unrestrained. No longer is this a form or effort but a natural response emanating from our hearts unto our Heavenly Father and our Lord Jesus, who we have long since come to know and love.

As we enter our retirement years as pillars of the church, we have the wonderful opportunity to bring stability and encouragement to the youth and younger adults who are emerging as church leaders. John the Baptist said that he had to become less and less, and Jesus more. We too must yield our roles to the younger men and women who have strong, proven abilities and the needed energy to carry the load.

Just as Elisha received the mantle of Elijah before Elijah was carried up to heaven, we must give over responsibilities to the younger men and women as they are trained, to assure vitality, continuity, and strength in the church.

Now, as firmly established in our hearts and minds over the many years each of us has walked with the Lord, his faithfulness and unconditional love continues to yield abundant and positive assurance that, no matter what happens, trust placed in him will always prosper.

Retirement, a more leisurely lifestyle, and catching up on hobbies and numerous projects which were always desired but never accomplished, is what most of us have waited to experience. It also affords time to renew acquaintances with many, and develop new friendships.

Therefore, purposeful planning with definite goals and objectives is needed to ensure that desire and discipline remain at an elevated level—especially during the first few years of this major change in what has been normal and routine living.

As people who have been Christians for most of their adult years, we are first God's servants and must not let ourselves drift into a life of inactivity, or one filled with our own selfish desires. Rather, we need to balance living by making ourselves available for teaching, counseling, exhorting, and comforting our Christian brothers and sisters, especially those new to the faith. We can also enjoy a lot of our own singular pleasures and recreational activities along the way. Balance is the key. We must be able to say *no* regarding some requests, but be open to saying *yes* regarding others.

Hopefully, most of us have sufficient financial resources at the time of retirement to allow us a certain latitude in our ability to travel, entertain, and make some unscheduled purchases—and still maintain a cheerful attitude regarding tithes and offerings unto the Lord through the local church.

As older folks, we find that most people are kinder and more respectful to us. We also find that instead of being the parents, the role has started to reverse, with our grown children showing parental concern for *our* well-being.

But this is to be anticipated and considered normal in the process of life. These golden years give us opportunities to love our family members unconditionally and with much enthusiasm. There should be no room for animosities, unforgiveness, or any other grievances. However, if any should remain, for whatever reasons, they should be taken to the Lord in prayer and then to the person or persons involved for loving resolution and reconciliation. This may not always be possible, but it should be prayerfully attempted. As Jesus told Peter in Matthew, chapter 18, when Peter asked,

> "Lord, how often should I forgive someone who sins against me? Seven times?" "No, not seven times," Jesus replied, "but seventy times seven!" (Matthew 18:21–22 NLT)

We must remember that unforgiveness presents a blockage to our relationships with the Lord, and our prayers will be hindered until we have done our part. The one who we have directly or indirectly offended may not accept our apology, but if we have asked in sincerity with true sorrow, God will be pleased and receive us once again, removing the barrier hindering our communications with him.

At this stage of our journey through life, any remnants of anger, bitterness, and unforgiveness are weights much too heavy for us to carry one more minute.

Therefore, it is so important to give them to God and allow his loving presence to waken our minds and hearts while encouraging and empowering us to initiate the restoration process regarding strained or broken relationships.

Therefore, let us proceed on to *the final victory.*

Chapter 9

THE FINAL VICTORY

"Look, I am coming soon! My reward is with me, and I will give to each person according to what they have done. I am the Alpha and the Omega, the First and the Last, the Beginning and the End." (Revelation 22:12–13 NIV)

For no one can lay any foundation other than the one already laid, which is Jesus Christ. If anyone builds on this foundation using gold, silver, costly stones, wood, hay or straw, their work will be shown for what it is, because the day will bring it to light. It will be revealed with fire, and the fire will test the quality of each person's work. If what he has built survives, he will receive his reward. If it is burned up, he will suffer loss; he himself will be saved but only as one escaping flames. (1 Corinthians 3:11–15 NIV)

Therefore, as we ponder our history after the many years have passed before us, we realize as never before that our time on earth has indeed been brief. Some will look back with great regret for wasted time and opportunities, while others will sense a rich fulfillment regarding family, friendships, and careers. However, for those who know Jesus as both Savior and Lord, the focal point of this latter chapter of life is a secure faith and trust in him and his promise of eternal life.

Sure, speculation is abundant on when and how we make the transition from physical beings of flesh and blood into spiritual beings brought face to face with the living God. However, we are assured through scripture that the Lord has gone to prepare a place for us so that when he returns, we will be with him forever.

Whether this is during our physical lifetime or through the grave, we have the confident assurance that it will be accomplished.

Revelation, chapter 7 tells us what the Lord promises believers in their eternal home.

> "[A]nd he who sits on the throne will shelter them with his presence. Never again will they hunger; never again will they thirst. The sun will not beat down on them, nor any scorching heat. For the Lamb at the center of the throne will be their shepherd; he will lead them to springs of living water. And God will wipe away every tear from their eyes." (Revelation 7:15–17 NIV)

Finally, in Matthew, chapter 6, Jesus teaches us,

> "That is why I tell you not to worry about everyday life—whether you have enough food and drink, or enough clothes to wear. Isn't life more than food, and your body more than clothing? Look at the birds. They don't plant or harvest or store food in barns, for your heavenly Father feeds them. And aren't you far more valuable to him than they are? Can all your worries add a single moment to your life? And why worry about your clothing? Look at the lilies of the field and how they grow. They don't work or make their clothing, yet Solomon in all his glory was not dressed as beautifully as they are. And if God cares so wonderfully for wildflowers that are here today and thrown into the fire tomorrow, he will certainly care for you. Why do you have so little faith? So, don't worry about these things, saying 'What will we eat? What will we drink? What will be wear?' These things dominate the thoughts of unbelievers, but your heavenly Father already knows all your needs. Seek the Kingdom of God above all else, and live righteously, and he will give you everything you need. So don't worry about tomorrow, for tomorrow will bring its own worries. Today's trouble is enough for today." (Matthew 6:25–34 NLT)

Jesus is not only our Savior, Lord, and friend, but he cares for all our needs and carries our burdens. Surely each of us has by now developed an intimate relationship of comfort and trust with him, and has learned to let him do so. Psalm 55:22 positively reinforces this.

> Give your burdens to the Lord and he will take care of you. He will not permit the godly to slip and fall. (Psalm 55:22 NLT)

The apostle Paul, as he was nearing the end of his life, declared in 2 Timothy, chapter 4,

> I have fought the good fight, I have finished the race, and I have remained faithful. And now the prize awaits me—the crown of righteousness which the Lord, the righteous Judge, will give me on the day of his return. *And the prize is not just for me but for all who eagerly look forward to his appearing.* (2 Timothy 4:7–8 NLT)

The road we traveled as we raced through life has now become history and scripture shows that a new road is laid out for us. Realizing this, our hearts cry out in eager anticipation as we continue to pursue the rich abundance and sweet comfort of God's Word knowing that *the final victory is at hand!*

Appendix

POWER FROM ON HIGH FOR THE BELIEVER

(Scriptures are from the New Living Translation Bible, New International Version, and New King James Version)
(Italics added for emphasis)

From attending Sunday school as children and church services as adults, we all heard and read the Bible passages regarding humankind's sins and that Jesus had died on a cruel cross, shedding his blood as full payment for them (John 3:16).

Also in John, chapter 3, we read about an old man named Nicodemus who came to speak to Jesus about the kingdom of God. Jesus simply replied,

> "I assure you, unless you are born again, you can never see the kingdom of God." (John 3:1 NLT)

From there we were shown scriptures known as the "Roman Road," or the steps to follow to be born again. These opened our understanding and increased our faith. In Romans, chapter 3 we read:

> For *all* have sinned; *all* fall short of God's glorious standard. Yet now God in his gracious kindness declares us not guilty. He has done this through Christ Jesus, who has freed us by taking away our sins.
>
> For God sent Jesus to take the punishment for our sins and to satisfy God's anger against us. We are made right with God when we believe that Jesus shed his blood, sacrificing his life for us. (Romans 3:23–25a NLT)

Romans 5:8 further explained:

> But God showed his love for us by sending Christ to die for us while we were yet sinners. (Romans 5:8 NLT)

Following along in Romans 6, the text declares:

> For the wages of sin is death, *but* the free gift of God is eternal life through Christ our Lord. (Romans 6:23 NLT)

Realizing then that everyone is a sinner, we looked at 1 John, chapter 1, which told us:

> If we say that we have no sin, we are only fooling ourselves and refusing to accept the truth. But if we confess our sins to him, he is *faithful and just* to forgive us and to cleanse us from every wrong. If we claim that we have not sinned, we are calling God a liar and showing that his word has no place in our hearts. (1 John 1:8–10 NLT)

Looking to what the Lord spoke to the church of Laodicea in Revelation chapter 3, we read:

> "Look! Here I stand at the door and knock. If you hear me (Jesus) calling and open the door, I will come in and we will share a meal as friends." (Revelation 3:20 NLT)

These are the doors of our hearts, and we learned we are the only ones who can open those doors to let him in. No one else can do that for us.

Finally, we saw in Romans, chapter 10 how we confirmed our faith in God through Christ Jesus.

> For if you confess *with your mouth* that Jesus is Lord and *believe in your heart* that God raised him from the dead, you *will* be saved. For it is *by believing in your heart* that you are made right with God, and it is by *confessing with your mouth that you are saved.* (Romans 10:9–10 NLT)

Romans, chapter 10 also encourages us.

> Yet faith comes from listening to this message of *good news—the Good News* about Christ. (Romans 10:17 NLT)

And in Hebrews 11, we are asked a question and then told the answer.

> What is faith? It is the confident assurance that what we hope for is going to happen. It is the evidence of things we cannot yet see. (Hebrews 11:1–2 NLT

Pondering these Scriptures, we continued growing in faith and realized we had become a "new creation" (2 Corinthians 5:17 NLT) by God's grace and love. It was also plainly revealed that by receiving Jesus as our Savior and Lord we were given the "gift" of the Holy Spirit.

In January 1963, my wife Donna and I received Jesus as our Savior and Lord during an altar call at a local church in Seattle, Washington, pastored by the late Rev. Dennis Bennett, who was well-known throughout the world in the charismatic movement of the 1960s.

After receiving Jesus as Savior and Lord, the person who had prayed with us shared the Scriptures regarding the "gift" of the Holy Spirit as expressed in the Books of Acts, Romans, and 1 Corinthians. Since the Holy Spirit was given to us as a "gift" when we received Jesus's salvation, this person asked us to pray to receive him by his baptism and explained how to do so.

In the Book of Acts, the descent of the Holy Spirit is described in chapter 2, as the disciples and other believers were praying together, and was manifested by them speaking in "tongues" * (other unknown languages) and prophesying. This occurred in AD 30 and included *all* of them there. Ten years later, in AD 40, Peter was guided by the Holy Spirit to share the gospel with a Gentile military man named Cornelius who was a captain of the Italian regiment (Acts 10).

Cornelius and his entire household received Jesus as Savior and Lord, and while they were praying, the Holy Spirit fell on them and they *all* spoke in tongues* and glorified God.

On the apostle Paul's third missionary journey in AD 54 (a full twenty-four years after the Holy Spirit came from heaven to earth), he traveled through the interior provinces and, when he came to Ephesus, he found several believers and said to them:

> "Did you receive the Holy Spirit when you believed?" "No," they replied, "We don't know what you mean. We haven't even heard that there is a Holy Spirit." "Then what baptism did you experience?" he asked. And they replied, "The baptism of John." Paul said "John's baptism was to demonstrate a desire to turn from sin to God. John himself told the people to believe in Jesus, the one John said would come later." As soon as they heard this, they were baptized in the name of Jesus. Then when Paul had laid hands on them, the Holy Spirit came on them, and they spoke in tongues* and prophesied. There were about 12 men in *all*. (Acts 19:2–7 NLT)

Some theologians have taught that the gifts of the Holy Spirit, including speaking in other tongues, died out after the time of the apostles. But the time frame listed above shows otherwise. The Holy Spirit came at Pentecost in AD 30 and is still in the world today as the believer's comforter and guide. Many say the same for the gift of speaking in other tongues. *

Above the Storm Clouds

However, 1 Corinthians, chapter 12 gives more detailed information on this.

> A spiritual gift is given to *each* of us as a means of helping the entire church. (1 Corinthians 12:7 NLT)

Another translation states verse 7 this way.

> To *each* is given the *manifestation* of the Holy Spirit for the common good. (1 Corinthians 12:7 NIV)

First Corinthians, chapter 13 gives further clarity on this.

> Love never fails. But whether there are prophecies, they will fail; whether there are tongues, * they will cease; whether there is knowledge, it will vanish away. For we know in part and we prophesy in part. *But when that which is perfect has come*, then that which is in part will be done away. When I was a child, I spoke as a child, I understood as a child, I thought as a child, but when I became a man, I put away childish things. For now, we see in a mirror, dimly, but then face to face. Now I know in part, but then I shall know just as I also am known. (1 Corinthians 13:8–12 NKJV)

Christian believers know that only Jesus is perfect, and when he returns, the imperfect will pass away. Has knowledge passed away? Of course not, because new discoveries are still found every day and become more amazing every year.

Therefore, until the perfect individual (Jesus) comes, prophecies and tongues will also remain valid if anointed and directed by the Holy Spirit.

The remainder of 1 Corinthians, chapter 12 further develops these gifts. However, *"the manifestation"* noted by Paul and the rest of the apostles was that *all* who were baptized in the Holy Spirit spoke in other tongues* (languages) and prophesied when they received Him.

As these various scriptures tell us, the baptism of the Holy Spirit is offered to all who have received Jesus as Savior and Lord of their lives. But this gift is established and His power is released as the believer, through a step of faith, is baptized in and by the Holy Spirit. In each case, as previously described, the tangible evidence is the speaking in unknown tongues* and/or prophesying.

Now if someone received one of the special gifts from the Holy Spirit, such as healing for instance, to use at will, it could soon fill that person with pride and arrogance. Paul tells us what God gave him in 2 Corinthians 12 because of his God-given gifts.

> But to keep me from getting puffed up, I was given a thorn in my flesh, a messenger of Satan to torment me and keep me from getting proud. (2 Corinthians 12:7 NLT)

The scripture seems to strongly infer that these gifts are given to a born again, Spirit-filled believer by God individually when needed to prevent that person from becoming puffed up.

My own experience speaking in unknown tongues* and witnessing this in many others gave me a private prayer language to bypass my mind. After running out of thoughts to express in my own language (English), I could pray more effectively from my spirit. But the Holy Spirit also can, by His anointing, urge me or other believers to speak out in our prayer language during a meeting with others present if that word is interpreted by the speaker or another who is also being anointed at the time with that gift. The apostle Paul tells us in 1 Corinthians 14:27 that

> No more than two or three should speak in tongues* (in a church meeting). They must speak one at a time, and someone must interpret what they say. But if no one is present who can interpret, they must be silent in your church meeting and speak in tongues to God Privately. (1 Corinthians 14:27 NLT)

Paul prefaces this in 1 Corinthians, chapter 14.

> I thank God that I speak in tongues* more than all of you. But in a church meeting I would much rather speak five understandable words that will help others than ten thousand words in an unknown language. (1 Corinthians 14:18 NLT)

Unfortunately, many churches today seem to have denied or subdued the power and guidance of the Holy Spirit, making their ministries weak. Sadly, many are *"having a form of Godliness but denying its power"* (2 Timothy 3:5 NKJV)

Almighty God, restore and revive your church in America and beyond and help all of us to seek the full power and guidance of the Holy Spirit. May he anoint your Word and make it come alive to all who diligently seek the truth! In Jesus's precious name, amen!

Addendum:

In one of his recent live-streamed sermons, Dr. Robert Morris, well-known pastor of the Gateway Church in Southlake, Texas, pointed out that there are three baptisms needed for the new believer.

The first is receiving Jesus as Savior and Lord at salvation through repentance of sins. The second is being baptized in water: a public declaration or outward sign of an inward work by the Lord Jesus. And third is the baptism of the Holy Spirit; the gift of the Holy Spirit, received at salvation, becomes active in the person when he or she asks Him to fill him or her with power and the anointing to understand Scripture and proceed forward with knowledge. He then gives the person a prayer language or unknown tongues* to allow him or her to speak from the heart to the Heavenly Father. He dispenses his other spiritual gifts as he sees fit to help and empower the new saint with the ability to boldly declare the good news of the gospel to the unsaved. His anointing thus helps build a strong faith, since faith comes by hearing and studying God's Word. The other gifts of the Holy Spirit (1 Corinthians 12:4–7) and the fruit of the Spirit (Galatians 5:22–23) are also manifested in each new believer (as God so desires) to honor and give glory to Him.

Steps to Help in Praying for the Baptism of the Holy Spirit

After reading the various verses listed above and meditating on them, the next step is to commune with God audibly, asking him to fill you with his Holy Spirit. After praying this request, start praising and thanking him for forgiving all your sins and saving you. Just close your eyes and spend some time praising and thanking him for these and his many other blessings. It is also an appropriate time to raise your hands as you honor him and surrender your will. As you tell him how much you love him and how much he means to you, you will soon sense his presence (or anointing) in the room around you. When this becomes apparent, stop praising him in the language you know and control with your mind and start to make sounds with your voice. As you do this in childlike faith, God will baptize you with his Holy Spirit and a sign of this will be the new language you are given. He will take the sounds you are making as a step of faith and allow you to speak in a distinct new language—one that comes from your heart (or spirit) and not your mind.

Continue praying with your mind of course, but also use your new language during your private prayer times; you will find many areas will be covered and questions answered beyond what you have even hoped for previously. Since scripture is only really understood by the illumination of the Holy Spirit, the Bible will come alive to you as never before. Remember, the Bible declares that we are the temples of the Holy Spirit. He lives in you and therefore can help, guide, and counsel, and give much wisdom for your daily living. Such requests of your Heavenly Father can be done in a public church setting, such as a Bible study or prayer meeting, but can also be undertaken while alone in the privacy of your home. God loves you and wants to strengthen and empower you for ministering the gospel message to others with confidence and much joy.

***Note:** Tongues is in the plural in both the KJV and Greek texts, meaning that the Holy Spirit can give a distinct new or different language to a believer if that is needed to get people's attention, as the disciples did when they all spoke in the upper room on the day of Pentecost (Acts 2:5–12 NLT).